CLOCKS!
HOW TIME FLIES

Table of Contents

CLOCKS!
HOW TIME FLIES

Siegfried Aust ▪ illustrated by Hans Poppel

Lerner Publications Company · Minneapolis

4 A Sense of Time

Children, come wash your hands. It's time for lunch!

Oh, is it that late already?

We're still nailing the boards

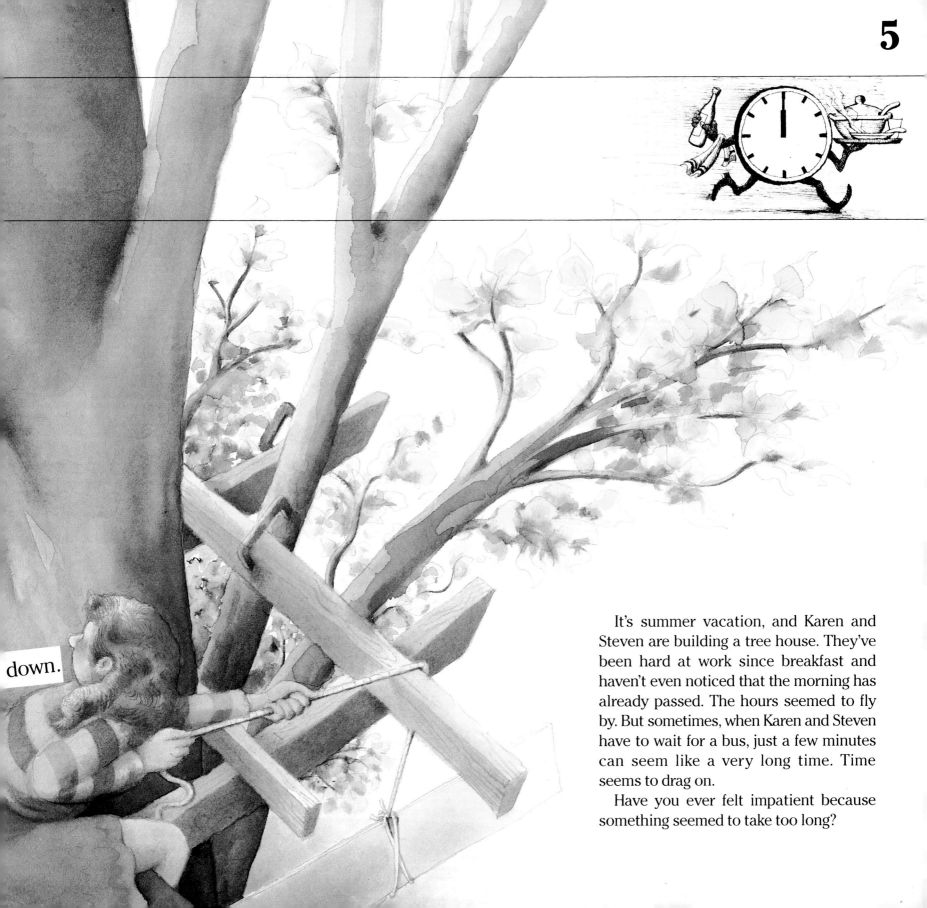

down.

It's summer vacation, and Karen and Steven are building a tree house. They've been hard at work since breakfast and haven't even noticed that the morning has already passed. The hours seemed to fly by. But sometimes, when Karen and Steven have to wait for a bus, just a few minutes can seem like a very long time. Time seems to drag on.

Have you ever felt impatient because something seemed to take too long?

6 The Natural Cycles of Time

Each circle shows a **cycle**—a series of activities that are repeated again and again.

The clock turns in a cycle.

Our daily cycle of activity

The seasons turn from one to the next in a yearly cycle.

The cycle of life from birth to death

This drawing shows a medieval farmer measuring time with his fingers and a piece of straw. He uses the straw's shadow to figure out where the sun is in the sky.

Before the invention of clocks and **watches,** people used the rhythms of nature as signals for the time of the day or the year. People planned their activities according to the rising and setting of the sun, the cycles of the moon, the growth of plants and crops, and the changing weather of the seasons.

In many places, people used bells to signal that it was time to wake up, work, eat, or sleep. In European churches, bells called people to their daily prayers.

People still use bells to organize the day. The school bell, for example, tells you when class begins and ends. In some factories, a siren or buzzer signals the beginning and end of the workday.

Even without a clock, you can estimate the time of day. The sun rises in the east, moves across the sky, and sets in the west. If you measure the length and direction of shadows cast by the sun, you can figure out how high the sun is in the sky and estimate the time of day.

Sundials were developed to track shadows in just the same way. Sundials come in many different shapes and sizes. All sundials have markings showing the hours of the day. As the sun moves across the sky, it casts a shadow across the sundial. The shadow moves from marking to marking, showing the time as the day goes by.

8 Sundials

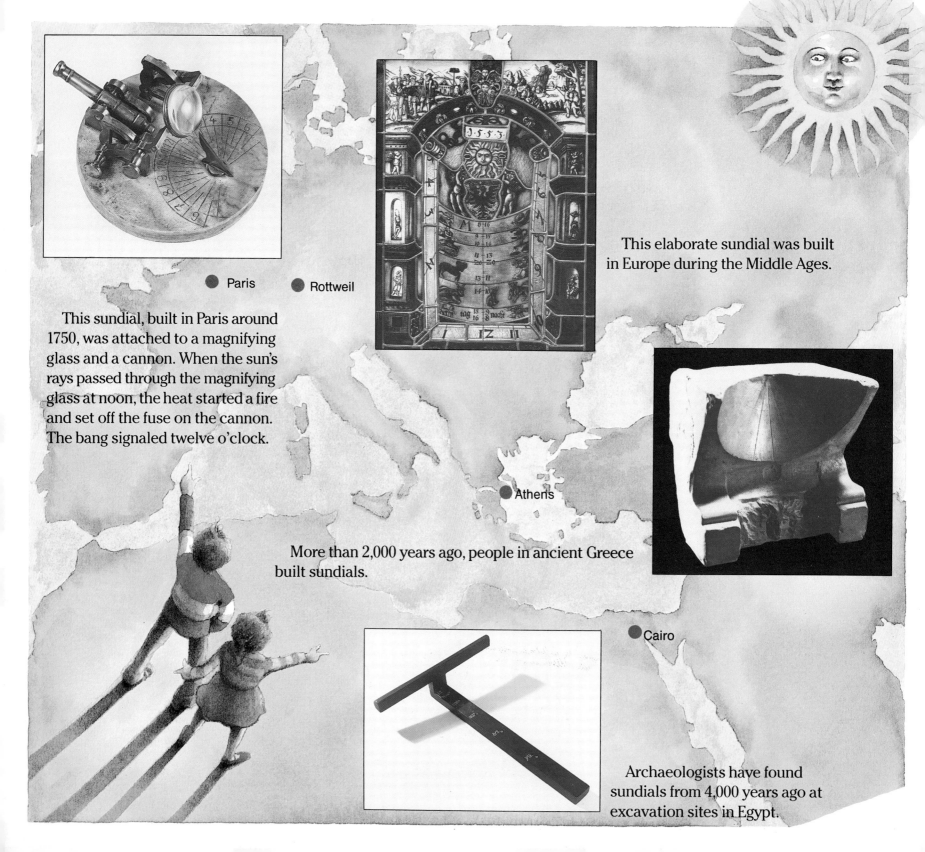

This sundial, built in Paris around 1750, was attached to a magnifying glass and a cannon. When the sun's rays passed through the magnifying glass at noon, the heat started a fire and set off the fuse on the cannon. The bang signaled twelve o'clock.

Paris

Rottweil

This elaborate sundial was built in Europe during the Middle Ages.

Athens

More than 2,000 years ago, people in ancient Greece built sundials.

Cairo

Archaeologists have found sundials from 4,000 years ago at excavation sites in Egypt.

You can build your own sundial. You will need a flowerpot filled with sand, a 12-inch (30-centimeter) stick, and some masking tape. Place the pot outside in the sun and set the stick in the middle of the sand.

Every hour, on the hour, take a piece of masking tape and mark the place where the shadow of the stick falls on the edge of the pot. Write the time on the tape. Now you can keep track of time on sunny days.

A statue with a sundial outside of the Strasbourg Cathedral in France

Most early sundials were found outside churches and homes. Some had beautiful fronts, or **faces.** The stick or post that casts the shadow on a sundial is called a **gnomon.**

The Roman numerals on this vertical sundial show the time of day.

Round, flat sundials measure the direction of shadows, while vertical, or upright, sundials measure the length of shadows. Between morning and noon, the shadow on a vertical sundial will grow shorter. From noon until evening, the shadow will become longer until the sun sets.

10 Water Clocks

People in ancient Egypt invented a way to measure time even when the sun was not shining. They developed a **water clock.** Some water clocks were "outflow clocks." They looked like decorated flowerpots with tiny holes in the sides. The pot would be filled with water, which would drip slowly through the holes.

Lines inside the pot showed how much time had passed as the water level sank.

Later, people developed "inflow clocks," such as the one shown below. With this clock, water dripped from the top container into the bottom container. The statue on the left is attached to a piece of cork that floats inside the bottom container. As the water level rises in the bottom container, the cork rises and so does the statue. The pointer in the statue's hand indicates the time of day.

Outflow and inflow clocks could be used to measure time indoors and after sunset.

You can make your own outflow clock with two empty cans. One can should be a little wider than the other.

Remove the tops of both cans and make a tiny hole in the bottom of the wider can.

Place the wide can on top of the narrow one. Pour some water into the top can and let the water drip through to the bottom can.

Every 15 minutes, draw a line inside the top can, right at the water level. Use a waterproof marker.

When all the water runs out of the top can, pour it back again. As the water drips through the hole again, you can watch the markings to tell when 15 minutes have passed.

Follow the diagram to build your own inflow clock.
1. Screw two big eye screws into a 12-inch (30-cm) wooden stick.
2. Pass a thin, round stick through the eye screws.
3. Insert the round stick into a piece of cork.
4. Fasten the wooden stick to a can with rubber bands.
5. Glue a cardboard arrow to the round stick so that it points to the wooden stick.
6. Make a tiny hole in the bottom corner of another can.
7. Fill the second can with water and set it on a platform so that water drips into the first can.
8. As the water rises in the bottom can, the cork will float higher and the arrow will move up.
9. Every 15 minutes, make a mark on the wooden stick where the arrow is pointing.
10. Fill the can again and watch the arrow keep track of the time.

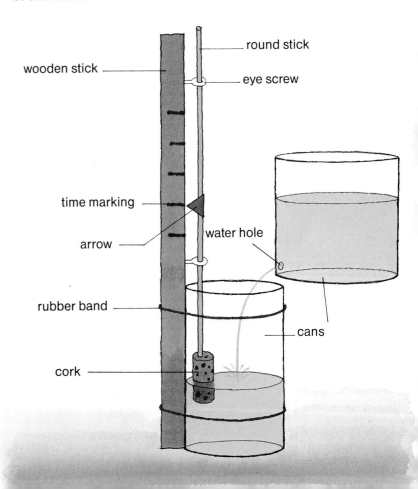

wooden stick — round stick — eye screw — time marking — arrow — water hole — rubber band — cans — cork

Sand Clocks and Hourglasses

On great sailing ships, sailors used to tell time with **sand clocks.** Water clocks would spill in rough seas, and sundials only worked during daylight hours. Sand clocks and other navigational instruments helped the sailors figure out their speed and location at sea.

Sand clocks were made of two glass bulbs connected by a narrow neck. The clocks were filled with fine, dry sand. The sand collected in the bottom glass bulb. When the sailors flipped the clock, the sand slowly streamed through the narrow middle portion. When all the sand had fallen to the bottom, the sailors knew a certain amount of time had passed. They flipped the clock and the measurement started again. Sand clocks that measured an hour became known as "hourglasses."

"Look at these beautiful hourglasses!"

"This one is from Italy…"

Let's Build a Sand Clock

Follow the instructions below to build your own sand clock. See how long it takes for the sand to run from one bottle into the other.

Get two glass bottles of equal size and fill one with sand.

Cut out a square of cardboard and poke a very small hole in it with a pencil.

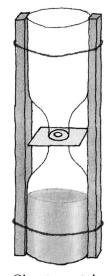

Glue the mouths of the bottles together with the cardboard in between.

Glue two strips of wood to the sides of the bottles and secure them with rubber bands. Flip the clock to begin your measurement.

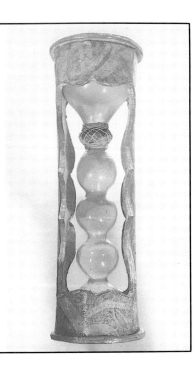

"...and this one's from France."

We still use sand clocks. You've probably seen a kitchen timer, a small sand clock that measures the time it takes to boil an egg.

Candle Clocks

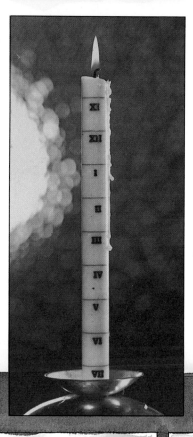

"Look at this candle with the numbers on it."

"It's a **candle clock** from England. As the candle burns down, it measures time."

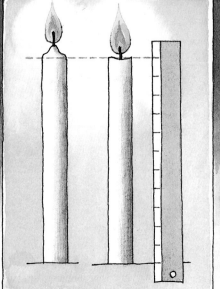

Light a household candle and let it burn down until the narrow tip is gone. Now measure the candle from the base to the top of the wax.

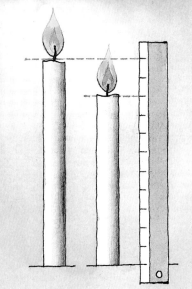

Let the candle burn for 10 minutes. Now measure it again. Subtract the second measurement from the first. This tells you how much of the candle burns every 10 minutes.

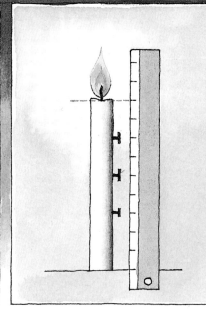

Mark off segments equal to 10 minutes each by pressing the tips of small metal thumbtacks into the candle.

Place the candle on a large metal dish. Now, as the candle burns down, the tacks will fall onto the plate and your clock will strike, or sound, every 10 minutes.

Mechanical clocks showed the time on a face, or **dial**. The word "dial" is derived from the Latin word *dies*, which means "day."

Early clocks were often ornate showpieces. Large mechanical clocks were placed outside church towers or city halls for everyone to see. Around 1344, one of the first large mechanical clocks was put up at the town hall in Padua, Italy.

Before people owned their own clocks, a watchman or timekeeper announced the time of day for all the townspeople. But during the Middle Ages, as businesses, churches, and governments became more organized, precision timekeeping became more important.

Except for the sundial, all the clocks we have discussed so far could only measure how much time had passed. They did not tell people the exact time of day. And although sundials told people the time of day, they were not very precise.

Mechanical clocks use gears, weights, chains, and springs to track time more accurately. The Chinese invented the first mechanical clock as long ago as 1088. During the mid-1300s, mechanical clocks came into everyday use. These clocks were more reliable and precise than sundials. They worked indoors and told the time during the day and night.

This machinery operated the large clock at St. Stephen's church in Vienna.

Mechanical Clocks

escapement

escape wheel

minute hand

gear wheel

minute wheel

hour hand

hour wheel

weight

pendulum

Pendulum clock with escapement and weight drive

Interlocking gears turn the wheels.

It is impossible to count all the drops of water in a flowing river. But it is possible to count drops that fall one after another from a dripping faucet. Time works the same way. When divided into small equal parts, or intervals, time can be measured precisely.

Mechanical clocks measure small intervals of time and track how much time has passed. To do this, the clocks must maintain a precise rhythm, so that each small measurement will be exactly the same.

The wheels and gears inside a mechanical clock are called **clockwork.** In some mechanical clocks, a heavy weight moves the clockwork. The weight is connected to a chain that is wound tightly around a drum. As the weight drops, the chain unwinds, the drum turns slowly, and all the wheels inside the clock move as well. As the wheels turn, they move the **hands**, or pointers, on the face of the clock.

The speed at which the weight and the wheels move is controlled by the swing of the clock's **pendulum.** As the pendulum swings, it moves a piece called an **escapement**. The escapement is connected to all the wheels in the clock, and it keeps the movement consistent and precise. With each small movement of the wheels, the hands of the clock inch along a bit farther.

When the weight in a mechanical clock drops and the chain unwinds as far as it will go, the clock stops. To start the clock you must rewind the chain and reset the weight.

Instead of a weight, some mechanical clocks and watches are powered by a coiled spring. As the spring uncoils, it works like a weight to move the clockwork. A **ratchet** works just like an escapement to regulate the movement of the wheels and gears. You must wind mechanical clocks regularly to keep them running.

Electric clocks became common in households in the 1920s. An electric current supplies the power and regulates the clock's speed.

The smallest electric clock motor is about as big as a ladybug.

Some old clocks were wound with a key.

Watches have a knob for winding the spring.

Some electric clocks are powered by batteries so they will be portable.

When the two gold weights fall as far as the chain allows, they must be pulled up again.

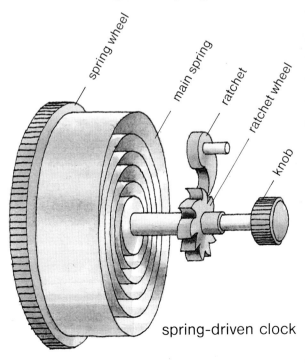

spring wheel
main spring
ratchet
ratchet wheel
knob

spring-driven clock

18 Dividing Time into Hours

This clock uses Roman numerals to mark the hours of the day. If you look closely you can see Arabic numerals that mark the 60 minutes of the hour. The long minute hand shows that it is 57 minutes past four o'clock. The short hour hand has almost reached the Roman numeral five.

The Babylonians began dividing time into intervals about 5,000 years ago. They divided the day into 24 parts, which we call hours. The 24-hour day was divided in two 12-hour portions: midnight to noon and noon to midnight.

The Babylonians also invented the 60-minute hour and the 360-degree circle. These measurements helped to build uniformity into daily life in Babylon.

Mechanical clocks of the Middle Ages also used the 24-hour divisions. The faces were divided into 12 equal parts, and the "hour hand" traveled around the dial. As clocks became more precise, clockmakers began to add "minute hands" that showed how many minutes had passed within an hour.

At midnight one day ends and a new day begins. Some say that midnight is the witching hour when all the spooks and ghosts come out.

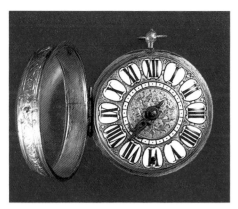

Clock faces may be plain or elaborate. This early clock has only an hour hand. There is no minute hand because the first clocks couldn't measure a minute precisely.

Modern clocks measure minutes as well as hours. The minute hand is always longer than the hour hand.

On many clocks, a third hand moves quickly around the dial. It moves about as fast as you can count "1001, 1002, 1003, 1004, 1005." It is the "second hand." There are 60 seconds in a minute.

Digital clocks do not have hands. They show the time with a numeral display. This clock shows **military time.** Military time counts the hours in a day from 1 to 24, instead of counting twice from 1 to 12. The time shown here is 16 hours, 17 minutes, and 56 seconds after midnight—that is, 4:17 in the afternoon.

20 Clocks for Use and Show

Some clocks have a gong or a chime that strikes on the hour. Some clocks chime every quarter of an hour.

In the tower of the Houses of Parliament in London, England, there is a very famous clock with a bell called "Big Ben." On the hour, Big Ben chimes the fifth bar of Handel's *Messiah*. The deep-toned bell rings every quarter hour as well.

In a cuckoo clock, a small wooden bird pops out of a door above the clock's face every hour and makes a "cuckoo" sound to announce the hour.

Wood carvers use themes from nature to make elaborate cuckoo clocks. The pinecones beneath the clock are actually the weights that operate the clockwork.

One of the most magnificent clocks in Germany was built in the tower of the Munich town hall in 1908. On the hour, the mechanical figures dance and sound instruments.

This "lamplighter clock" announces the hour by lighting a match. On the hour, the figure's hand flips up and strikes the match against the edge of the matchbox.

930562

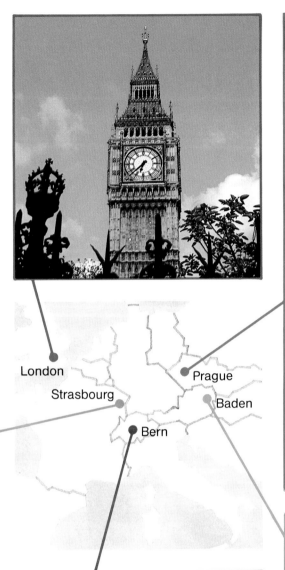

Some clocks are famous because of their beauty and size. Pictured here are Big Ben in London, the Prague Clock in Prague, Czechoslovakia, a flower clock in Baden, Austria, the Zytglogge in Bern, Switzerland, and an astronomical clock in Strasbourg, France.

London
Strasbourg
Prague
Baden
Bern

The astronomical clock tells the hour, the minute, and the second, the positions of the sun and the stars, the position and phase of the moon, and the day, the month, and the year.

Essential Clocks in Our Day

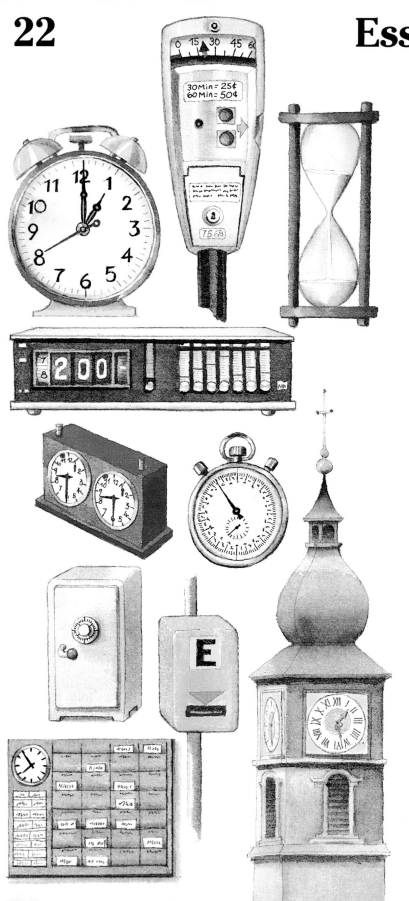

Some clocks do more than just tell time. Many clocks tell people when to begin or end a specific activity. Find the following clocks in the picture:

In the morning, the *alarm clock* wakes us with a bell or buzzer.

The *church clock* rings when the service begins.

The *time clock* keeps track of when people come to work and when they leave for the day.

At some parking lots, a *time stamper* punches a ticket to show the amount of time your car has been parked at the lot.

A *time-lock safe* protects valuables from burglars. The safe can only be opened at certain times.

A *digital clock* doesn't have hands.

Using a *stopwatch*, you can measure how fast you can run.

A *parking meter* shows how long you can leave your car in a parking space.

A *chess clock* tells the chess player how much time he or she has to make the next move.

A *kitchen timer* uses sand to show how long eggs should cook.

In the modern world, people need special clocks to help them keep on schedule each day. You can buy a clock radio with an alarm. Instead of a noisy buzzer or bell, the clock radio will wake you with music or a news broadcast from your favorite radio station.

Some people have coffeemakers with built-in clocks. They set the machine to begin brewing coffee just before they want to wake up in the morning, so that a hot pot of coffee will be ready.

Video cassette recorders have clocks that help you record your favorite T.V. show. You can leave the house and the VCR will automatically begin taping the show at just the right time.

Peter Henlein, a clockmaker from Nuremberg, Germany, is said to have built the first clock that people could carry in their pockets. It was called a "pocket watch."

Henlein's watch could run for 40 hours without having to be rewound. Some pocket watches struck the hour. Others had ornate covers for the dials. Some were adorned with jewels or were worn on a chain.

Over time, pocket watches became smaller and simpler. In the 1860s, women began to wear watches attached to bracelets.

During the First World War, soldiers found that watches worn on a wristband were easy to use in the field. Since then, the **wristwatch** has become popular all over the world.

Some wristwatches tell not only the time of day but also the day, the month, and the year. You can even buy wristwatches with built-in alarms and calculators.

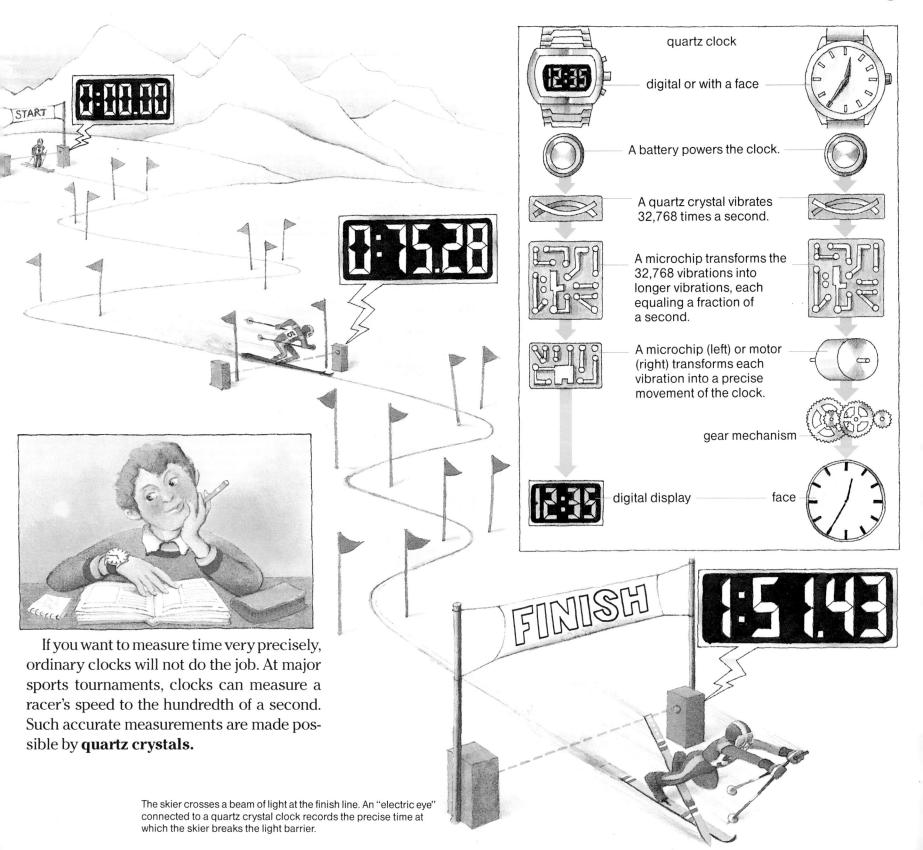

quartz clock

digital or with a face

A battery powers the clock.

A quartz crystal vibrates 32,768 times a second.

A microchip transforms the 32,768 vibrations into longer vibrations, each equaling a fraction of a second.

A microchip (left) or motor (right) transforms each vibration into a precise movement of the clock.

gear mechanism

digital display · · · · · · · face

If you want to measure time very precisely, ordinary clocks will not do the job. At major sports tournaments, clocks can measure a racer's speed to the hundredth of a second. Such accurate measurements are made possible by **quartz crystals.**

The skier crosses a beam of light at the finish line. An "electric eye" connected to a quartz crystal clock records the precise time at which the skier breaks the light barrier.

26 Atomic Clocks

Atomic clocks use atoms to tell time. These atoms oscillate (move back and forth) billions of times per second. The rhythm is so precise that atomic clocks are accurate to within a few **nanoseconds** per day. A nanosecond equals one billionth of a second.

The atomic clock at the United States Naval Observatory in Washington, D.C., is one of 50 atomic clocks in the world.

Does your clock keep accurate time? Test it. All you need to do is compare the time shown on your clock with the time announced on the radio.

You can also call a local telephone number to find out the exact time. The phone number should be listed in your telephone book.

Telephone time announcements are set to **atomic clocks** that run with the utmost precision.

The atomic clock at the Physical-Technical State Institute, Braunschweig, Germany

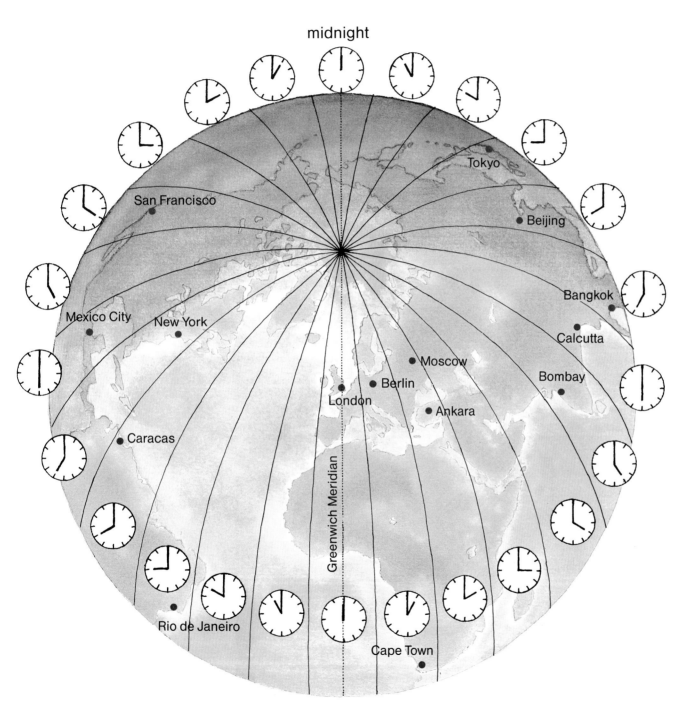

midnight

Tokyo

San Francisco

Beijing

Mexico City   New York

Bangkok

Calcutta

Moscow

Berlin

Bombay

London

Ankara

Caracas

Greenwich Meridian

Rio de Janeiro

Cape Town

noon

When people are getting up for breakfast in New York, people in Germany are preparing for lunch. How come?

Since the Earth rotates, night falls on one half of the world while day occurs in the other half. Looking at this map you can see the time differences at locations all around the world. Each clock shows a different **time zone.** There are 24 time zones in the world, just as there are 24 hours in a day. Large countries, like the United States, have more than one time zone.

In 1884, the meridian, or longitude line, that runs through Greenwich, England, was established as the starting point for the 24 time zones.

Twice a year, we change the time on our clocks to make better use of daylight and thus conserve energy. In spring, we set the clocks forward one hour to "daylight saving time." In fall, we set the clocks back an hour to "standard time."

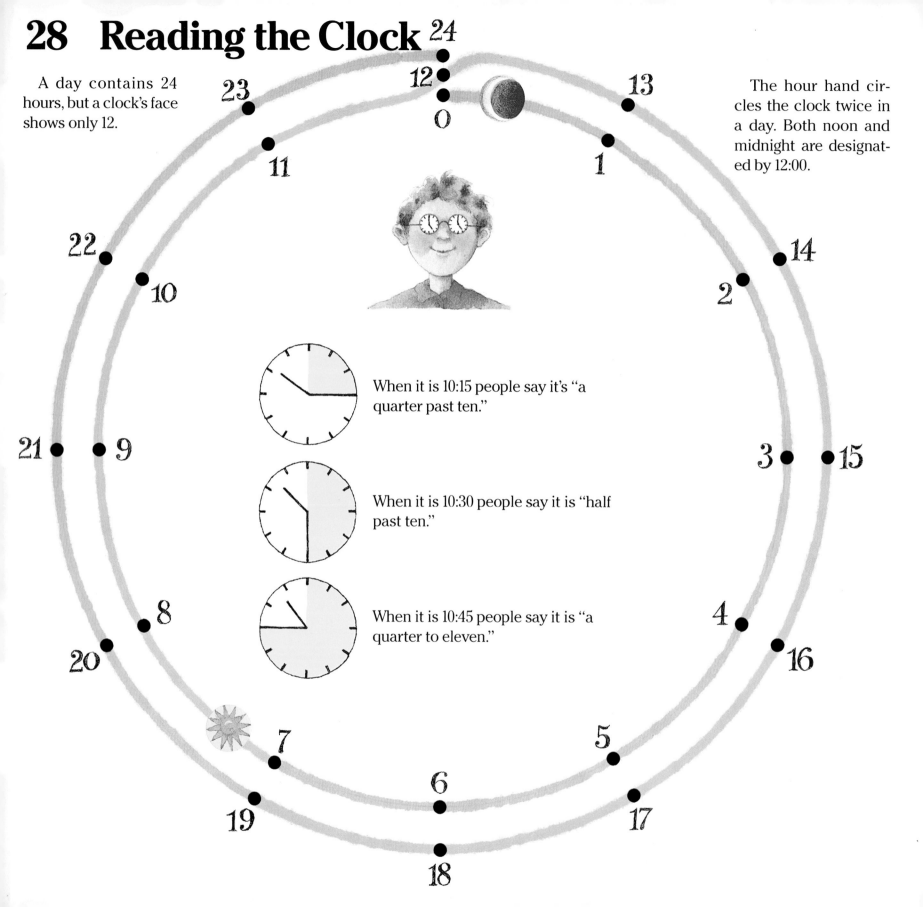

A day contains 24 hours, but a clock's face shows only 12.

The hour hand circles the clock twice in a day. Both noon and midnight are designated by 12:00.

When it is 10:15 people say it's "a quarter past ten."

When it is 10:30 people say it is "half past ten."

When it is 10:45 people say it is "a quarter to eleven."

If you've ever traveled by airplane or waited for a friend at the airport, you know you must check the digital display monitors to find out if the flight is on time.

Each airline has a monitor that lists the flights that are scheduled to arrive and depart that day. The chart tells when an incoming flight is *supposed* to arrive, and then it shows the *actual* arrival time if the flight has been delayed. The chart also shows whether your airplane will depart on time or not. Occasionally, airplanes arrive early, but they never depart before the scheduled time.

You can find time schedules in bus stations and train stations too.

30 Clock Repair

When clocks don't run properly, they need to be fixed by a clockmaker or jeweler. Modern clockmakers rarely make clocks themselves. Usually they just repair clocks that were made in factories.

The clockmaker's tools include a special magnifying glass. The glass helps the clockmaker to see the tiny wheels and gears inside a clock.

You can make your own mechanical clock from a kit. Clock kits are available at hobby shops.

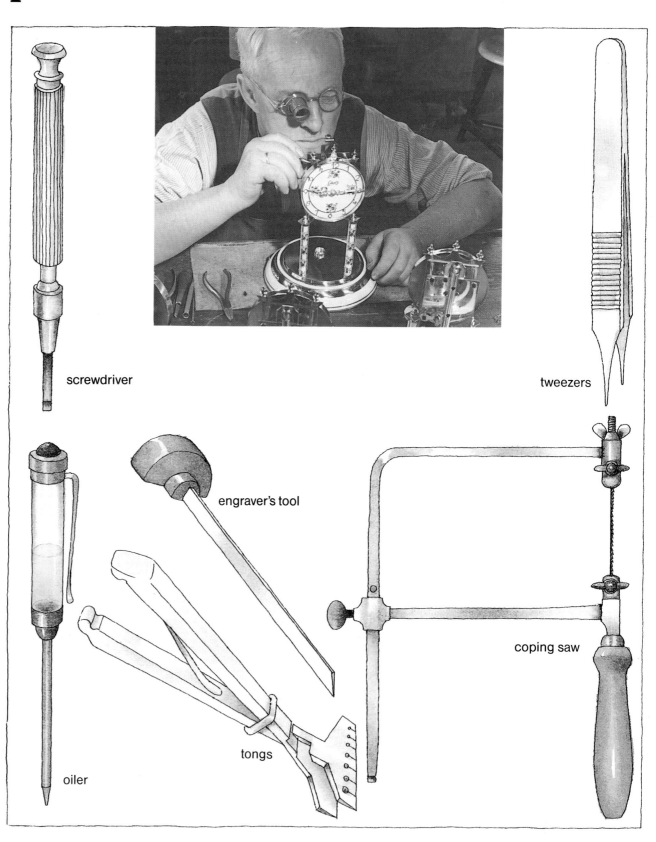

screwdriver

tweezers

engraver's tool

coping saw

tongs

oiler

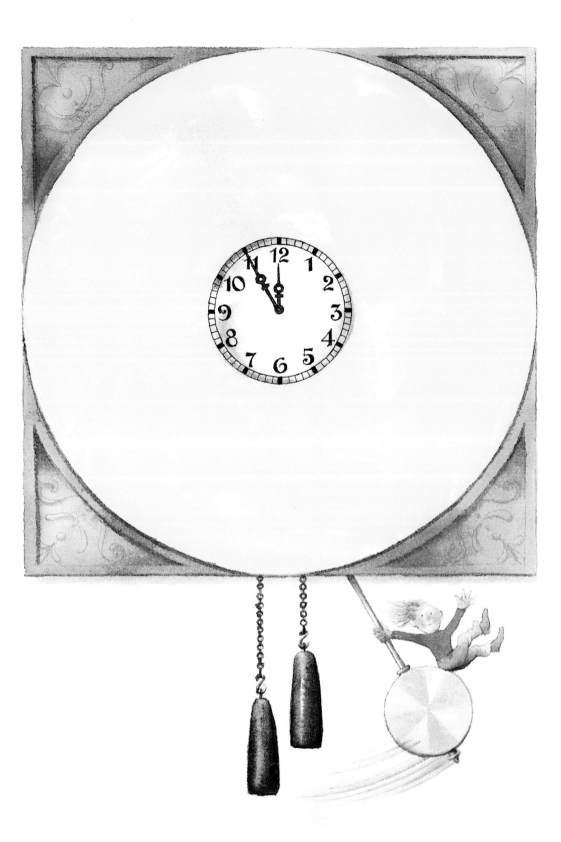

Acknowledgments

Photographs courtesy of: Verlag Carl Ueber-reuter, pp. 7, 9 (right), 17 (bottom left); Wuppertal Clock Museum, pp. 8, 10 (right), 12, 13 (left), 14, 20 (center); Anton Lubke, pp. 9 (left), 21 (left, bottom center), 30 (top); Science Museum, London, p. 10 (left); Jerome Rogers, pp. 13 (right), 23 (top), 29 (bottom); Historical Museum of Vienna, pp. 15, 17 (top left); German Clock Museum, Furtwangen-Schwartzwald, pp. 17 (top right, bottom right), 19 (top and bottom), 24 (top left); Rijksmuseum-Stichting, Amsterdam, p. 18; Selva Engineering, Trossingen, pp. 19 (second photo from bottom), 30 (left); German Clock Industry Union, Pforzheim, pp. 19 (second from top), 20 (top right); Suddeutscher Verlag, Munich, p. 20 (left); British Foreign Service Office, Vienna, p. 21 (top); Township of Baden, p. 21 (bottom right); Karel Plicka, Prague, p. 21 (top right); Black & Decker, p. 23 (bottom left); Zenith Electronics Corporation, p. 23 (bottom right); National Maritime Museum, London, p. 24 (top right); Hantor Warenhandel, p. 24 (bottom left); Trustees of the British Museum, London, p. 24 (bottom right); Physical-Technical State Institute, Braunschweig, p. 26; Experimental Aircraft Association, p. 29 (top).

Author Siegfried Aust loves both technology and writing for children. Aust has combined his interests in the Fun with Technology series. He is a teacher who has written many books for young readers.

Illustrator Hans Poppel has many talents. He plays jazz piano and has worked as a stage designer. Poppel now devotes his time to illustrating books for both children and adults.

This edition first published 1991 by Lerner Publications Company. All English language rights reserved.

Original edition copyright © 1984 by Verlag Carl Ueberreuter, Vienna, under the title Kinder, wie die Zeit vergeht: von Uhren und anderen Zeitmessern. Translation copyright © 1991 by Lerner Publications Company. Translated from the German by Amy Gelman. Additional text and illustrations copyright © 1991 by Lerner Publications.

Library of Congress Cataloging-in-Publication Data

Aust, Siegfried.
  [Kinder, wie die Zeit vergeht. English]
  Clocks! : how time flies / Siegfried Aust ; illustrated by Hans Poppel.
     p.   cm.
  Translation of: Kinder, wie die Zeit vergeht.
  Summary: Discusses time, the invention of clocks to keep track of daily activities, and types of clocks from sundial and water clock to electric and atomic clocks.
  ISBN 0-8225-2154-7 (lib. bdg.)
  1. Time—Juvenile literature. 2. Astronomical clocks—Juvenile literature. 3. Clocks and watches—Juvenile literature. [1. Time. 2. Clocks and watches.] I. Poppel, Hans. ill. II. Title. III. Title: How time flies.
QB209.5.A96   1991
529—dc20
                                                             90-26569
                                                                CIP
                                                                 AC

Manufactured in the United States of America

1 2 3 4 5 6 7 8 9 10 00 99 98 97 96 95 94 93 92 91